A TRUE BOOK™

DIY DO IT YOURSELF

Amazing Makerspace
# Movers

## KRISTINA A. HOLZWEISS

**Children's Press®**
An Imprint of Scholastic Inc.

D062000B

**Content Consultant**
Shaunna Smith, EdD
Assistant Professor of Educational Technology
Department of Curriculum
Texas State University, San Marcos, Texas

Library of Congress Cataloging-in-Publication Data
Names: Holzweiss, Kristina A.
Title: Amazing makerspace DIY movers / by Kristina A. Holzweiss.
Description: New York : Children's Press, 2018. | Series: A true book | Includes bibliographical
   references and index.
Identifiers: LCCN 2016052794| ISBN 9780531238479 (library binding : alk. paper) |
   ISBN 9780531240984 (pbk. : alk. paper)
Subjects: LCSH: Motion—Juvenile literature. | Handicraft—Juvenile literature.
Classification: LCC QC127.4 .H65 2018 | DDC 531/.112078—dc23
LC record available at https://lccn.loc.gov/2016052794

SCHOLASTIC, CHILDREN'S PRESS, A TRUE BOOK™, and associated logos are trademarks and/or
registered trademarks of Scholastic Inc., 557 Broadway, New York, NY 10012.
1 2 3 4 5 6 7 8 9 10 R 27 26 25 24 23 22 21 20 19 18

**Front cover: Speedboat project**

**Back cover: Students with Speedboat
and Pendulum projects**

# Find the Truth!

**Everything** you are about to read is true *except* for one of the sentences on this page.

Which one is **TRUE**?

**T or F**   Electricity is the universe's only form of energy.

**T or F**   Energy cannot be destroyed.

Find the answers in this book.

# Contents

You Can Be a Maker! ................ 6

## 1 Start Your Engines!

What is the difference between
potential and kinetic energy? ................. 9

## 2 Speedboat

Why do boats float? .......................... 19

THE **BIG** TRUTH!

## Leonardo da Vinci's Workshop: The Original Makerspace

What are some inventions that
Leonardo da Vinci designed? ............... 28

Solar-powered fan

People on this ride
feel centripetal force.

**3** Solar-Powered Fan

How can the sun spin a fan?................. **31**

Famous Inventors
and Pioneers......................... **40**

Timeline ............................. **42**

True Statistics.............. **44**

Resources ................. **45**

Important Words............ **46**

Index ..................... **47**

About the Author........... **48**

**Warning!**
Some of these projects use pointy,
sticky, hot, or otherwise risky objects.
Keep a trusted adult around to
help you out and keep you safe.

# You Can Be a Maker!

Makers are always thinking about problems and searching for ways to solve them. These problem solvers create machines and test them out. Then they think about what they have learned and improve their work.

You can be a maker, too! This book will help you create things that move. Follow the directions to make these machines in a **makerspace**. Then experiment with your creations to make them even better!

Solar-powered fan

Speedboat

Pendulum

# ThinkAhead!
## What makes a pendulum swing back and forth?

# CHAPTER 1

# Start Your Engines!

Pendulums are simple devices. They may keep time or just provide entertainment. You've been on a pendulum if you've ever ridden on a swing. You can see a pendulum tick back and forth on a grandfather clock. You can also create a pendulum of your own! All you'll need are a few basic supplies. You can probably find these materials around a makerspace.

 Pendulums can make exciting amusement park rides!

When you stretch a rubber band, it has potential energy. When you let it go, the potential energy turns into kinetic energy as the rubber band flies through the air.

# Potential and Kinetic Energy

All machines need energy to work. When you hold a pendulum to the side, energy is stored inside it, waiting to be released. This energy is called **potential energy**. When you release the pendulum, it moves. The potential energy has become **kinetic energy**. Energy can transform from one form to another, but it can't be destroyed.

People on this ride feel centripetal force as they swing around in a circle.

# Centripetal Force

A force is something that changes an object's movement. An object in motion, or with **velocity**, naturally travels in a straight line. It takes an additional force to make that line curve. This is where centripetal force comes in. It pulls objects toward a central point, or **axis**. On a pendulum, the axis is the point from which the pendulum swings. The twine pulls the washers to that axis. This forces the washers in a curved path. If you were to swing the pendulum all the way around, the washers would travel in  a circular path.

11

# Swinging Pendulum

## What You Need

A half circle (like this protractor) is 180 degrees. A full circle is 360 degrees.

- [ ] Pencil
- [ ] Paper
- [ ] Thin hardcover book
- [ ] Sturdy, flat surface, such as a table or desk
- [ ] Protractor
- [ ] Tape
- [ ] 2 to 3 heavy books, such as textbooks (optional)
- [ ] 10 metal washers
- [ ] 2 feet (0.6 meters) of twine
- [ ] Ruler
- [ ] Stopwatch or a watch with a second hand

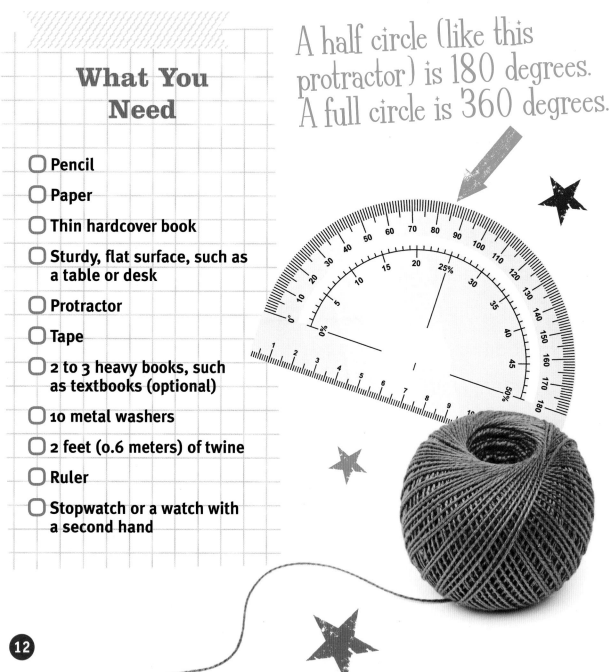

# Project Instructions

1. On your paper, create a chart that looks like the one below. You'll record this information for each time you swing your pendulum.

| Pendulum length | Number of Washers | Angle of Swing | Time per Swing |
|---|---|---|---|
| | | | |

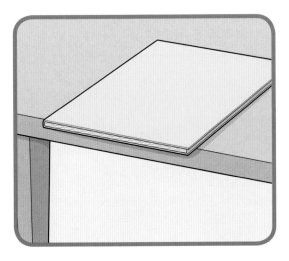

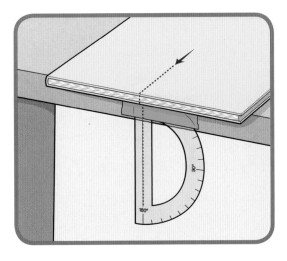

2. Set the thin hardcover book on a flat surface, such as a table. Position the book so about 0.25 inch (0.6 centimeters) hangs over the edge of the table.

3. Tape the protractor to the end of the table as shown so one edge is flush against the book. Make sure the protractor's 0/180 degree line is centered below the book.

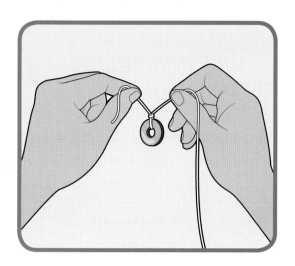

**4.** Tie one metal washer securely to one end of the twine.

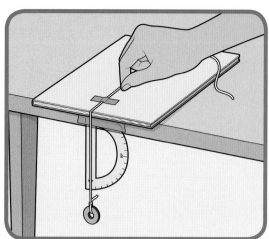

**5.** Lay the other end of the twine across the book on the table. Tape it down to the book to keep it in place.

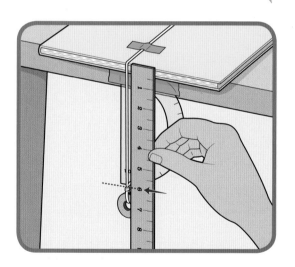

**6.** Use the ruler to make sure 6 inches (15.2 cm) of twine hangs over the edge of the book and down to the floor.

**7.** Line the twine up with the 0/180 degree line on the protractor. If you want, set some books on top of the twine. It will help keep the twine in place.

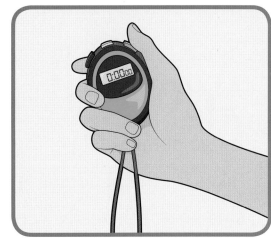

**8.** Hold the washer at the end of the twine. Move it to the side so the twine lies along the 10 degree mark on the protractor.

**9.** Get your stopwatch or watch ready!

Adding books on top of the twine keeps the pendulum more strongly in place, but you don't need them.

# Move It and Test It!

Let go of the washer. Count the number of seconds it takes for the pendulum to make one full swing, to one side and back again. Record the results on your chart.

Repeat it a few times. First, change the number of washers on the pendulum. After that, try making the pendulum longer or shorter. Change the angle of the swing to 20, 30, or more degrees on the next try. Record all of your results on your chart. What patterns do you notice?

# Change It!

You can create art with your pendulum.

Create a stronger support from which to hang your pendulum. Use a yardstick or similar object and tape it to the tabletop with duct tape. Next, use two pieces of string instead of one to make your pendulum. Poke a hole in the bottom of a small plastic or paper cup. Attach the cup to the ends of the two strings with tape. Lay a large piece of paper below. Pour some watered-down tempera paint into the cup. Now swing your pendulum gently and watch it create a beautiful design below. (This project is best done outside!)

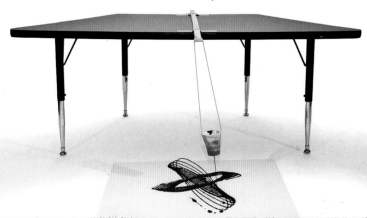

# Think Ahead!

Where will potential energy be stored on this boat?

# CHAPTER 2

# Speedboat

People have been building boats for at least 10,000 years. The earliest boats relied on human passengers to row or paddle them across the water. Later, inventors found ways to add powerful engines. This helped boats move faster. For this maker creation, you'll build your own tiny speedboat. In this case, a rubber band will provide the power. Let's find out how.

Americans own nearly 12 million recreational boats, or boats used just for fun.

# Buoyancy

For a boat to work, it needs to be able to float. This ability is called buoyancy. An object's **buoyancy** depends in part on its density, or how closely packed its atoms and molecules are. The more closely packed the atoms, the denser the object is. If the object is less dense than water, it floats. If it is denser than water, it sinks. And the denser it is, the faster and deeper it sinks.

**A boat's shape and the materials it is made from help give it buoyancy.**

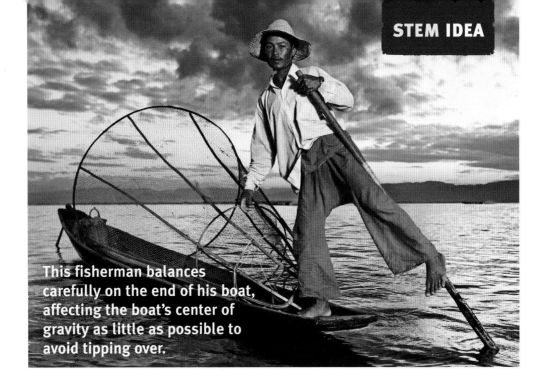

This fisherman balances carefully on the end of his boat, affecting the boat's center of gravity as little as possible to avoid tipping over.

# Center of Gravity

Have you ever been in a small boat? When you moved around, you probably felt the boat move, too. You might have needed to be careful to avoid tipping the boat over. When you moved, you were changing the boat's center of gravity. This is the point around which an object's **mass** is balanced. The higher an object's center of gravity is above a surface, the easier it is for it to tip over.

# Build a Speedboat

## What You Need

- ○ 2-liter plastic soda bottle, clean, with the cap on
- ○ 2 wooden dowels, each roughly 12 inches (30.5 cm) long
- ○ Duct tape
- ○ 2 plastic spoons
- ○ Scissors
- ○ Hot glue gun and glue sticks
- ○ Strong rubber band wide enough to wrap around the soda bottle
- ○ Waterproof markers
- ○ Pennies

## Project Instructions

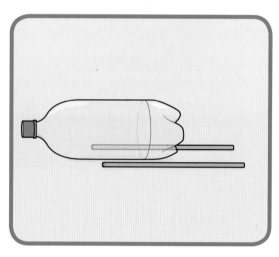

**1.** Position the dowels lengthwise along the outside of the bottle, on opposite sides. They should stick out past the bottom of the bottle by about half their length.

22

You can discard the parts of the handles you cut off. Keep the round parts of the spoons.

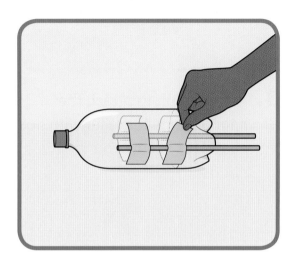

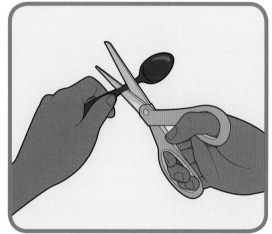

**2.** Attach them to the bottle with plenty of duct tape.

**3.** Using scissors, cut off most of the handles of the two spoons, leaving 1 inch (2.5 cm) of the handle below the round part.

**4.** Lay the stems of the spoons on top of each other. Point the round parts in opposite directions. Make sure the round part of one spoon faces up and the other faces down.

**5.** Ask an adult to attach the spoon stems together with hot glue. This is now your boat's paddle.

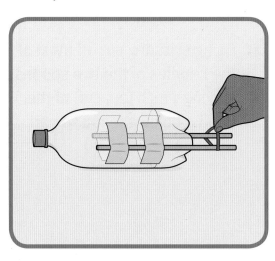

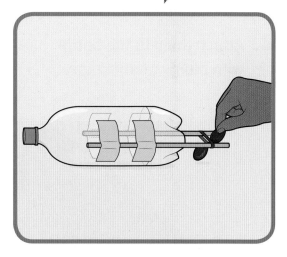

**6.** Loop the rubber band so it wraps around both ends of the dowels until it is snug.

**7.** Insert the spoon paddle through the rubber band.

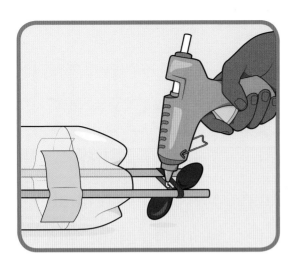

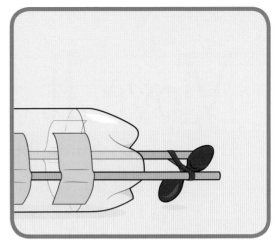

**8.** Ask an adult to attach the center of the spoon paddle to the rubber band with hot glue.

**9.** Make sure the glue is dry and everything is connected securely.

Ink from waterproof markers won't wash off when you put your boat in the water.

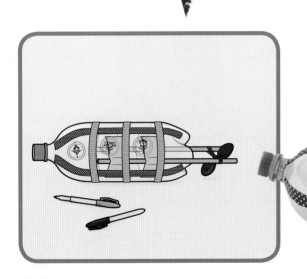

**10.** Decorate the soda bottle with waterproof markers.

# Move It and Test It!

Wind the paddle until the rubber band is stretched as far as it will go. This will build up a lot of potential energy. While holding the twisted paddle in place, put the boat in a swimming pool or bathtub. Let go of the paddle, allowing the kinetic energy to flow. Watch your boat zoom away. Now place some pennies inside the bottom of your boat and try again. How many pennies can your boat hold and still move forward?

# Change It!

With some experimentation, your boat might be able to carry more pennies. You may also find ways to make it move more quickly or more slowly. Try building your boat in different ways. Which changes do you think will work best? Test them out. What differences do you notice, and why do you think they occur?

- Use a milk jug, juice carton, or soda can instead of a 2-liter bottle.
- Change the size of the spoons you use for your paddle.
- Use chopsticks, pencils, or paint stirrers instead of dowels.

1 Tbs
15 ml

1/2 Tbs
7.5 ml

1 tsp
5 ml

1/2 tsp
2.5 ml

1/4 tsp
1.25 ml

# Leonardo da Vinci's Workshop: The Original Makerspace

Leonardo da Vinci (1452–1519) is perhaps most famous for his art. However, he was also a writer, musician, architect, engineer, scientist, mathematician, and inventor. Leonardo filled many notebooks with plans for incredible machines. He didn't build many of them, but his ideas have inspired several remarkable inventions.

### Helicopter
Leonardo sketched an idea for a helicopter-like flying vehicle. It had a corkscrew-shaped blade that would lift the vehicle into the air as it spun.

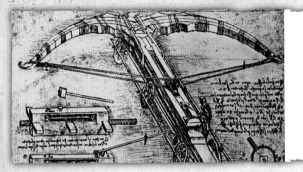

## Giant crossbow

Leonardo's giant crossbow was designed to be 42.7 feet (13 meters) wide. It was mounted on six wheels so it could be moved around easily.

## Parachute

Leonardo designed a pyramid-shaped parachute. It was to be built by stretching cloth around a wooden frame.

## SCUBA gear

Leonardo's diving gear idea involved a mask with long tubes and a floating device that kept the tubes' ends above the water.

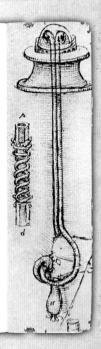

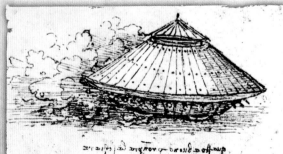

## Armored tank

Leonardo imagined a war vehicle. It had a circular platform with sloped, armored sides. Cannons would fire from its sides.

# Think Ahead!

**What do you think makes air move?**

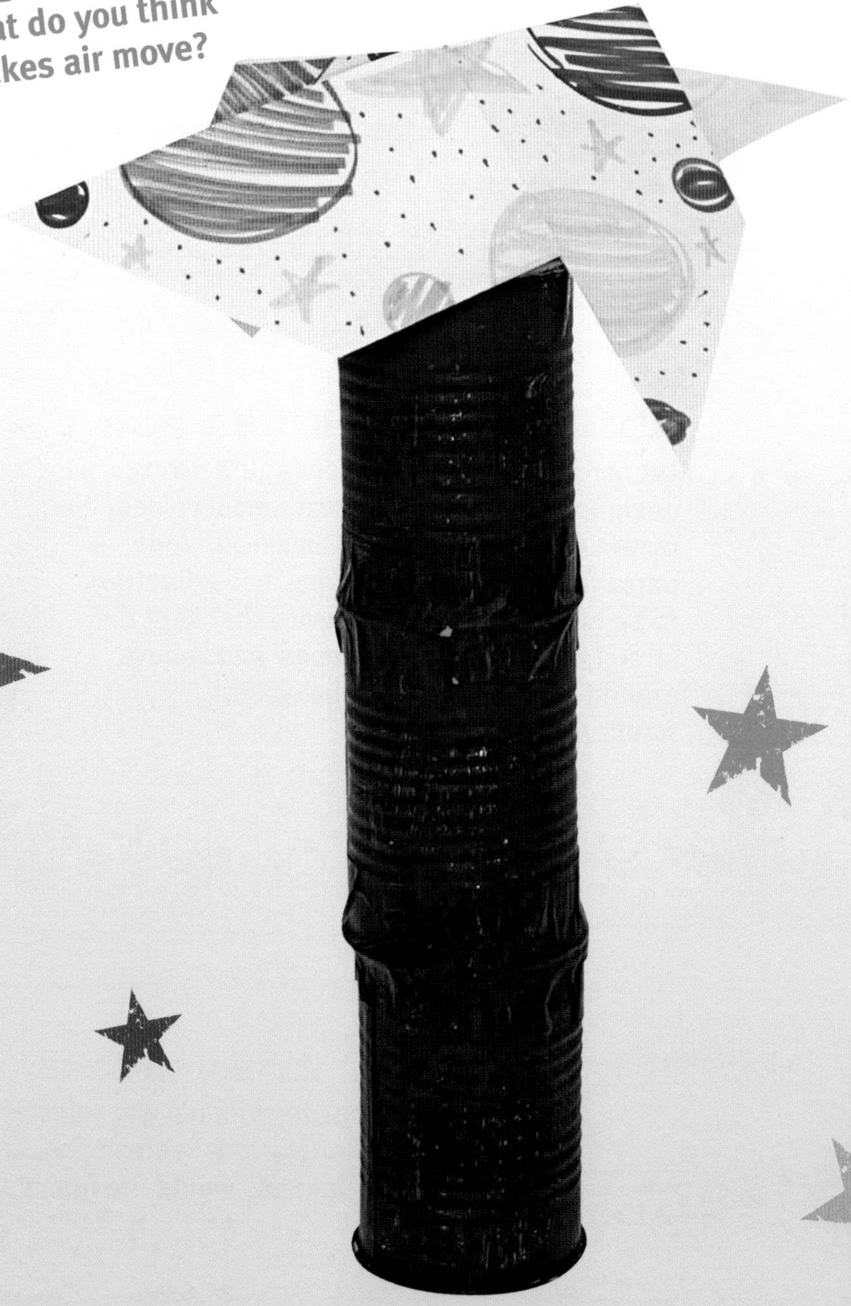

# Solar-Powered Fan

Electric fans were invented in the 1880s. These devices have curved or angled blades that spin in a circle. Electricity powers the fan and moves the blades in a circle. The shape of the blades pulls air in from one side and pushes it out the other. In this project, you will use some maker creativity to build a fan of your own. This fan won't need electricity. Instead of the fan blades moving the air, the air will move the blades.

The first electric fan was invented in the 1880s.

# Temperature and Air Movement

When air warms, it rises. When it cools, it sinks. These air movements will drive your solar fan. Metal cans will form the base of the fan. When sunlight heats the cans, the air inside will warm up and rise. As the air moves out the top of the cans, it will flow across your fan blades and make them spin. New air will be pulled through the bottom of the cans and then heated. The continuous **circulation** of air will keep the fan spinning.

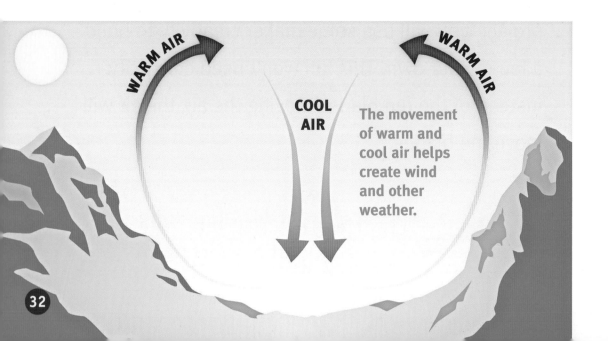

WARM AIR

WARM AIR

COOL AIR

The movement of warm and cool air helps create wind and other weather.

# Friction

With inventions that move, you must consider **friction**. This force fights against motion when objects slide against each other. If you slide a box across the floor, friction with the floor slows and stops the box. In this project, you will balance fan blades on a thumbtack. Because the fan only touches the tip of the tack, it slides against a tiny area. Therefore, there is very little friction. This makes it easy for the fan to spin.

The friction between an object and the ground can make it hard to slide a heavy object across a floor.

HANDLE WITH CARE

1set

33

# Build a Solar-Powered Fan

## What You Need

- [ ] 3 clean, empty metal cans, such as soup or vegetable cans, of the same size
- [ ] Can opener
- [ ] Duct tape
- [ ] Black paint (acrylic paint is a good choice)
- [ ] Paintbrush
- [ ] Large wire paper clip
- [ ] Thumbtack
- [ ] 8.5-inch (21.6 cm) square piece of white paper (or a regular sheet of printer or notebook paper)

- [ ] Markers, crayons,or colored pencils
- [ ] Ruler
- [ ] Pencil
- [ ] Scissors
- [ ] Clear tape
- [ ] 2 books of the same thickness
- [ ] Sunshine

# Project Instructions

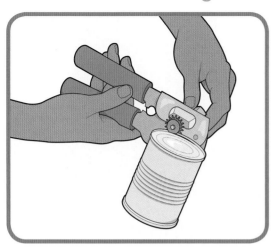

**1.** Ask an adult to help you use the can opener to remove the tops and bottoms of all three cans.

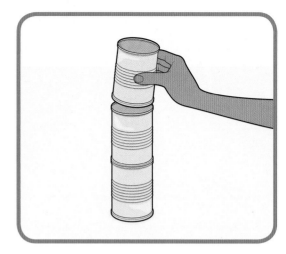

**2.** Stack the cans on top of each other.

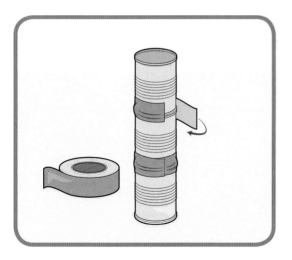

**3.** Connect the edges of the cans with duct tape, forming a tower.

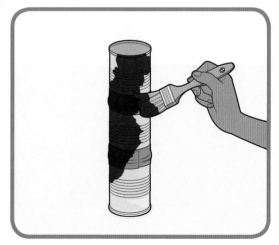

**4.** Use the paint and brush to paint the tower black. Let the paint dry.

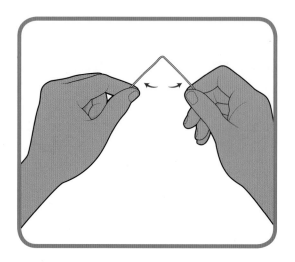

**5.** Unwind the paper clip until it is completely straight. Then bend it to create an arch shape.

**6.** Attach the ends of the paper clip arch to the top of the tower with duct tape.

**7.** Attach the thumbtack to the very top of the arch with duct tape. The point should face up.

**8.** Decorate the paper with markers, crayons, or colored pencils. Be creative!

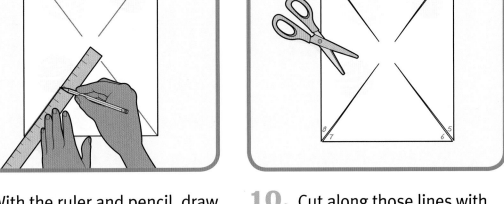

**9.** With the ruler and pencil, draw lines 5.75 inches (14.6 cm) long from each corner toward the center of the paper.

**10.** Cut along those lines with scissors. This will make 8 separate points. Number each point 1 through 8 with a pencil.

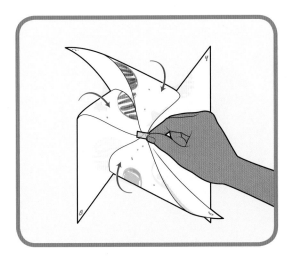

**11.** Bend points 1, 3, 5, and 7 to the center of the paper. Tape the folded pieces down. This creates your fan.

**12.** Lay the books about 3 inches (7.6 cm) away from each other on a level surface in direct sunlight.

# Move It and Test It!

Set the tower on the books so that it sits above the gap between the books. This will allow air to flow in from underneath. Balance the paper fan blades on the point of the thumbtack. Heat from the sun will warm the air inside the tower, making the air rise and turn the fan. If it isn't working, check the fan. If the blades are unevenly sized or one side droops, you may need to adjust the fan or remake it. ★

# Change It!

Try building this project different ways. How do you think each change will affect your fan? What results do you actually notice? Why do you think the changes, if there are any, occur?

- Paint the tower white or another light color.
- Use black paper for the fan blades.
- Make the fan out of heavier paper or even a different material.
- Set the tower on a higher stack of books.

# Famous Inventors and Pioneers

## Stephen Perry

**(?–?)** In 1845, British inventor Stephen Perry used stretchy rubber—a recent discovery at the time—to create the first rubber bands. At first, rubber bands were used mainly in factories. Since then, they have become common household items.

## Karl Benz

**(1844–1929)** Karl Benz was a German engineer and inventor who created the world's first practical automobile in 1885. Benz's earliest car designs had three wheels. He later switched to the four-wheeled style most cars use today. The Mercedes-Benz automobile company still bears his name today.

## Schuyler Skaats Wheeler

**(1860–1923)** Schuyler Skaats Wheeler was an American inventor who created the first electric fan in the 1880s. Wheeler's design had two blades. Since then, inventors have created countless variations on his original model.

## Igor Sikorsky

**(1889–1972)** Igor Sikorsky was a Russian-American inventor who helped design many types of aircraft in the 20th century. He is best known for creating the world's first widely used helicopters during the 1930s and '40s.

## Henry Ford

**(1863–1947)** Like Karl Benz, American inventor and businessman Henry Ford was an early pioneer in the automobile industry. He is

perhaps most famous for his use of the assembly line, which allowed his company to build cars more quickly than anyone had before.

## Dean Kamen

**(1951– )** Dean Kamen is an American inventor who worked on projects in a wide range of fields. In 2001, he showed off a new invention called the Segway. It is a type of scooter that allows users to travel quickly without much physical effort. Segways make it easy to travel short distances in a city and are often used by tour groups.

# Timeline

**Christiaan Huygens invents a clock that is controlled by a swinging pendulum.**

| About 250 BCE | 1656 CE | 1680s |
|---|---|---|

**Archimedes describes his principle of buoyancy.**

**English scientist and mathematician Sir Isaac Newton outlines his three laws of motion, which remain a key part of the study of physics today.**

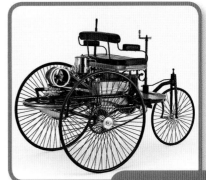

French scientist Alexandre-Edmond Becquerel makes the world's first solar cell, leading to later advances in solar energy.

Karl Benz builds the world's first practical automobile.

**1807** > **1839** > **1880s** > **1885** >

Schuyler Skaats Wheeler invents the electric fan.

Inventor Robert Fulton builds the first successful steam-powered boat.

# True Statistics

**Length of the Seawise Giant, the largest ship ever built:** 1,500 feet (457 m)

**Width of the Seawise Giant:** 226 feet (69 m)

**World record speed for a boat:** 317.6 miles per hour (511.13 kilometers per hour)

**Percentage of electricity in the United States generated from solar power:** 0.6

**Distance sunlight travels to reach Earth:** 92.9 million miles (149.5 million km)

## Did you find the truth?

**F** Electricity is the universe's only form of energy.

**T** Energy cannot be destroyed.

# Resources

## Books

Gray, Susan Heinrichs. *Experiments with Motion*. New York: Children's Press, 2012.

Gregory, Josh. *Henry Ford: Father of the Auto Industry*. New York: Children's Press, 2014.

Hakim, Joy. *The Story of Science: Newton at the Center*. Washington, DC: Smithsonian Books, 2005.

Roslund, Samantha, and Emily Puckett Rodgers. *Makerspaces*. Ann Arbor, MI: Cherry Lake Publishing, 2014.

**Visit this Scholastic website for more information on movers:**

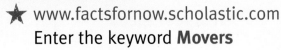 www.factsfornow.scholastic.com
Enter the keyword **Movers**

# Important Words

**axis** (AK-sis) an imaginary line through the middle of an object, around which that object spins

**buoyancy** (BOI-uhn-see) the ability to float

**circulation** (sur-kyuh-LAY-shuhn) the continuous movement around something, or from one point to another and back

**friction** (FRIK-shuhn) the force that slows down objects when they rub against each other

**kinetic energy** (ki-NET-ik EN-ur-jee) energy that has to do with motion

**makerspace** (MAY-kur-spays) any place where people plan, design, tinker, create, change, and fix things for fun or to solve problems

**mass** (MAS) the amount of physical matter that an object contains

**potential energy** (puh-TEN-shuhl EN-ur-jee) energy contained within an object that the object is not yet using

**velocity** (vuh-LAH-si-tee) speed

# Index

Page numbers in **bold** indicate illustrations.

air movement, **32**
Archimedes, **42**
atoms, 20
automobiles, 40, 41, **43**
axis, 11

Benz, Karl, **40**, 43
boats, 19, **20, 21, 43**
buoyancy, **20**, 42

center of gravity, **21**
centripetal force, 11
circulation, **32**
crossbow, **29**

density, 20

electricity, 31

fans, 31, **41**, 43
Ford, Henry, **41**
friction, **33**
Fulton, Robert, 43

helicopter, **28, 41**
Huygens, Christiaan, **42**

Kamen, Dean, **41**
kinetic energy, 10, 26

laws of motion, 42
Leonardo da Vinci, 28–29

makers, 6
mass, 21
molecules, 20

Newton, Sir Isaac, **42**

parachute, **29**
pendulums, 9, 10, 11, 42
Perry, Stephen, 40
physics, 42
potential energy, 10, 26

rubber bands, 19, 26, **40**

SCUBA gear, **29**
Segway scooter, **41**
Sikorsky, Igor, **41**
solar cells, 43
Solar-Powered Fan project
    assembly, 35–37
    design alterations, 39
    materials, 34
    testing, 38
Speedboat project
    assembly, 22–25
    design alterations, 27
    materials, 22
    rubber band, 26
    testing, 26
steam-powered boats, **43**
Swinging Pendulum project
    art with, 17
    assembly, 13–15
    chart, 13
    design alterations, 17
    materials, 12
    testing, 16

tank, **29**
temperatures, **32**

velocity, 11

Wheeler, Schuyler Skaats, 41, 43

# About the Author

Kristina A. Holzweiss was selected by *School Library Journal* as the School Librarian of the Year in 2015. She is the founder of SLIME—Students of Long Island Maker Expo—and the president of Long Island LEADS, a nonprofit organization to promote STEAM education and the maker movement. In her free time, Kristina enjoys making memories with her husband, Mike, and their three children, Tyler, Riley, and Lexy.

Scholastic Library Publishing wants to especially thank Kristina A. Holzweiss, Bay Shore Middle School, and all the kids who worked as models in these books for their time and generosity.

**PHOTOGRAPHS** ©: Education Images/UIG/Getty Images; 5 markers and throughout: photosync/Shutterstock; 5 colored papers and throughout: MNI/Shutterstock; 8: Justin Chin/Bloomberg/Getty Images; 10: Ian Lishman/Getty Images; 11: Education Images/UIG/Getty Images; 12 graph paper and throughout: billnoll/iStockphoto; 12 top right: Melodist/Shutterstock; 12 bottom right: Yellowj/Shutterstock; 13 pencil and throughout: Vitaly Zorkin/Shutterstock; 17: Jennifer A. Uihlein; 20: Daniel Grill/Getty Images; 21: hadynyah/Getty Images; 22 bottom: james westman/Shutterstock; 23 bottom: Lubava/Shutterstock; 26 water: Yeryomina Anastassiya/Shutterstock; 27: Dave King Dorling Kindersley/Getty Images; 28: ART Collection/Alamy Images; 29 top: PRISMA ARCHIVO/Alamy Images; 29 bottom: INTERFOTO/Alamy Images; 29 center right: Sheila Terry/Science Source; 29 center left: Robin Treadwell/Science Source; 32: Encyclopaedia Britannica/UIG/Getty Images; 33: SIBSA Digital Pvt. Ltd./Alamy Images; 38 background: Triff/Shutterstock; 39: Tarzhanova/iStockphoto; 40 left: JaggedPixels/iStockphoto; 40 right: Hulton-Deutsch Collection/CORBIS/Getty Images; 41 top: From Appletons' Cyclopedia of Applied Mechanics/Internet Archive Book/Flickr; 41 center right: Library of Congress/digital version by Science Faction/Getty Images; 41 center left: Keystone-France/Getty Images; 41 bottom: Mark Peterson/Corbis/Getty Images; 42 bottom left: Mary Evans Picture Library Ltd./age fotostock; 42 bottom right: National Geographic Stock: Vintage Collection/The Granger Collection; 42 top: Science History Images/Alamy Images; 43 bottom left: The Granger Collection; 43 top left: Apic/Getty Images; 43 top right: National Motor Museum/Heritage Images/Getty Images; 43 bottom right: From Appletons' Cyclopedia of Applied Mechanics/Internet Archive Book/Flickr; 44: Ian Lishman/Getty Images.

All instructional illustrations by Brown Bird Design.
All other images by Bianca Alexis Photography.